Isaac Newton & His Laws of Motion

by Mona Chiang

Table of Contents

Introduction	2
Chapter 1 Who Was Isaac Newton?	4
Chapter 2 Newton's First Law of Motion	8
Chapter 3 Newton's Second Law of Motion	16
Chapter 4 Newton's Third Law of Motion	24
Conclusion	28
Solve This Answers	30
Glossary	31
Index	32

Introduction

You're playing in a championship basketball game. You have the ball and dribble it up the court. Then the strangest thought pops into your head. Why does the ball always bounce back up after it hits the floor?

You're still thinking about this as you jump to take a shot. The ball arcs up to the basket, then down . . . and totally misses the backboard, rim, and even the net. Airball! Now you wonder, "Why can't I jump so high that I fly above the hoop? Why do things move the way they do?"

People have been asking those same questions for a long time. But no one had a good explanation until the late 1600s. That's when an English scientist named Isaac Newton came up with some answers. He developed a set of laws, or guiding principles, about motion that have influenced science for centuries.

▲ **Isaac Newton lived from 1642 to 1727.**

Newton's laws use math to explain how everything moves. They even help explain why the planets in the solar system **orbit**, or move around the sun. As you read, you'll learn about these laws. You'll discover how these laws work in the world around you.

1. Solve This

Length of Time it Takes to Orbit the Sun

Planet	Time in Earth Years
Mercury	0.24
Venus	0.62
Earth	1
Mars	1.88
Jupiter	11.86
Saturn	29.46
Uranus	84.01
Neptune	164.8
Pluto	247.7

Math ✓ point

Explain how you can estimate to solve each problem.

Use the table above to answer the following questions.

a. Pluto's orbit is almost three times as long as which planet's orbit?

b. About how many Earth days does it take for Mercury to complete one orbit?

CHAPTER 1

Who Was Isaac Newton?

Isaac Newton was born in England in 1642. His father, also named Isaac, was a farmer who could not read or write. He died three months before his son was born. When Isaac was three, his mother, Hannah, married a wealthy preacher from a nearby village. He sent Isaac to live with his grandparents.

When Isaac was ten years old, his mother sent him away to school. At first, Isaac's teachers placed him at the bottom of his class. But he quickly became the top student. Isaac also became known at school for his strange inventions. Once he made a tiny, wooden windmill powered by a running mouse.

▲ Newton was born at Woolsthorpe Manor in the village of Woolsthorpe, England.

Isaac continued his education at Trinity College, Cambridge. To pay for his schooling, he had to work as a servant for wealthy students.

Although he studied many subjects, mathematics and **optics**, the science of light, interested him the most. Isaac sometimes studied so hard that he forgot to eat or sleep. Later, Newton became a teacher at Trinity College.

2. Solve This

Isaac is walking his horse. He is busy thinking about sunlight, and the horse runs off. Isaac continues to walk in a straight line, but the horse gallops away at a 75° angle.
a. Draw the angle formed as Isaac and the horse move away from one another.
b. What type of angle is formed?

Math ✓ point

Explain how you know the angle you drew was 75 degrees.

3. Solve This

Study the map of England to answer the following question.
About how far is it from Woolsthorpe, in the center of the circle, to London?

Math ✓ point

What tool do you need to solve this problem?

CHAPTER 1

Man of Many Sciences

Isaac Newton made several key discoveries. He is most famous for his work on **force**, motion, and **gravity** (GRAHV-ih-tee). Gravity is a force that pulls objects toward Earth. That's why you can't fly above a basketball hoop for a slam-dunk.

To better understand gravity, Newton first studied what other scientists had learned about it. Then he studied their ideas on how the planets orbit the sun. He thought the two problems were related. By making observations and thinking, Isaac came up with the law of universal gravitation.

This law explains that all objects in the universe have gravity. Newton was the first to recognize that the force holding any object to Earth is the same as the force holding the moon and planets in their orbits. Newton used his knowledge of optics to build a powerful telescope called the reflecting telescope.

▼ For his many accomplishments, including the invention of the reflecting telescope, Newton was awarded knighthood. He became known as Sir Isaac Newton.

Myth or Reality?

There's a myth that Newton "discovered" gravity when an apple fell on his head while he slept under an apple tree. Boink! The idea of gravity hit him along with the apple. But Newton said that ideas did not come to him quickly. He had to think long and hard—often for years—before he solved a problem.

4. Solve This

Weight is actually the measurement of the force of gravity on an object. For example, your weight measures how much gravity is pulling on your body. Since not all planets have the same gravitational pull, an object will weigh different amounts throughout the solar system.

Use the gravity factors in the table to answer the following questions.
a. If an elephant weighs 10,000 pounds on Earth, how much would it weigh on Uranus?
b. How much would an elephant weigh on Earth if it weighs 722 pounds on Mars?

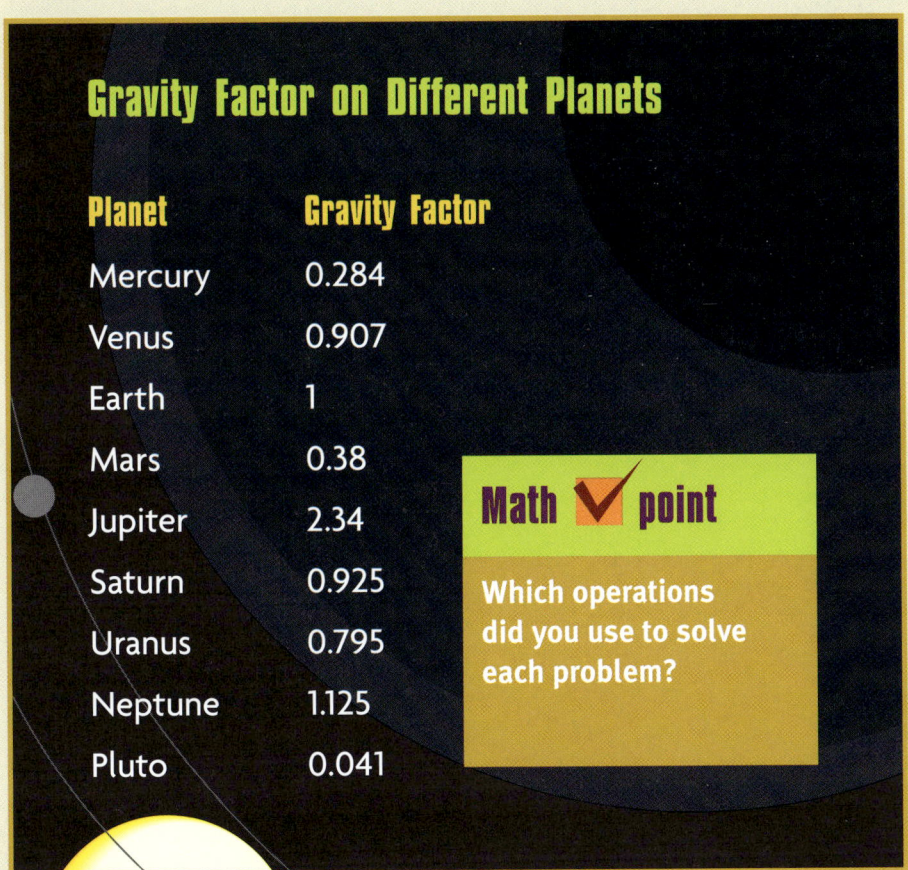

Gravity Factor on Different Planets

Planet	Gravity Factor
Mercury	0.284
Venus	0.907
Earth	1
Mars	0.38
Jupiter	2.34
Saturn	0.925
Uranus	0.795
Neptune	1.125
Pluto	0.041

Math point

Which operations did you use to solve each problem?

CHAPTER 2

Newton's First Law of Motion

Push a ball along the ground. Your push is a force that makes the ball move. The ball rolls, slows down, and comes to a stop. Why does it stop? If you lived before Isaac Newton's time, you would probably say the ball ran out of force. But that changed in the late 1500s.

An Italian scientist named Galileo Galilei (gah-lih-LEE-oh gah-lih-LAY) conducted many experiments to test new ideas about motion. He rolled balls down ramps, swung objects back and forth, and dropped objects from different heights. He made careful observations and measurements during each experiment. Finally, Galileo came to a surprising conclusion: A moving object does not need anything to keep it moving. The object will slow down and stop only when another force slows it and stops it.

When Newton was in college, he studied Galileo's work on motion. He knew that Galileo had the right idea. Newton improved on Galileo's idea and stated it as the first law of motion.

Galileo was one of the first people to do experiments to test his ideas. ▼

First Law of Motion

An object that is at rest, or not moving, will stay at rest until a force acts on it. A moving object will continue moving at the same speed and in the same direction unless a force acts on it.

CHAPTER 2

The First Law in Action

Let's head to a soccer field to see the first law of motion in action. A soccer ball sits on the field. The ball can't move by itself; it needs a force to make it move. Where does the force come from? A soccer player's foot pushes the ball and gets it rolling. That's the first part of the law.

Then, as the ball rolls, it slows down. The player has to keep kicking the ball to keep it going. But according to the second part of the law, the ball should keep moving at the same **speed**—unless a force acts on it. Aha! That last phrase is the key point. A force is acting on the ball. **Friction** (FRIK-shuhn) with the grass and particles in the air slows the ball down. Friction is a force that occurs whenever two objects rub against each other.

▲ The force of a kick makes the ball move.

10

NEWTON'S FIRST LAW OF MOTION

Everyday Science

You are sitting in the front seat of a car on the passenger (right-hand) side. The car turns left. What happens? You end up pushed against the door. Why? Newton's first law of motion! You were moving forward along with the car. The car turns left, but you are not part of the car. So you continue moving forward until the inside of the car door pushes against you.

CHAPTER 2

Other Forces

During a soccer game, other forces change a ball's motion, too. The force of gravity pulls the ball down. Kicks on different sides of the ball make it zigzag up the field.

Of course, Newton's first law applies to more than soccer, and forces come in other forms. For instance, wind is a force that makes a sailboat change direction. Your legs pedaling a bicycle provide the force that makes it speed up.

Now think about any change in motion. What force or forces might cause those changes?

▲ Wind is a force that makes a sailboat change direction.

NEWTON'S FIRST LAW OF MOTION

Everyday Science

Two balls of the same **mass,** or amount of matter, are kicked with the same force. One ball is kicked across a grass playing field. The other is kicked across the pavement (which provides much less friction than grass). Both surfaces are flat. Which ball will stop its motion first?

▼ A force acts on the ball to change its direction, speed, or both.

CHAPTER 2

The First Law and Space Travel

Friction and gravity affect just about every object on Earth. If you could somehow turn off these forces, a moving object would keep moving at the same speed in the same direction even if you didn't add any force. That's exactly what happens in space travel.

Think about a space probe going to Mars. Once the rocket escapes Earth's gravity, the engines are shut down. Outer space has no air particles to cause friction. So the spacecraft zooms straight ahead even without added power. Only a force, such as the firing of rocket engines, will change the spacecraft's motion.

▲ Space probes move as Newton's first law of motion predicts.

NEWTON'S FIRST LAW OF MOTION

A Stubborn Thing Called Inertia

Newton's first law shows that an object will not change its motion unless a force acts on it. In other words, an object resists any change in its motion. This resistance is called **inertia** (ih-NUR-shuh). The more mass an object has, the more inertia it has. A truck has more inertia than a small car. Therefore, a truck needs more force to overcome its inertia and change its motion.

Hands-on Experiment

Put an index card on top of a plastic cup. Place a coin on the index card. Pull the card away quickly. What happens to the coin? How did the coin's inertia affect what happened?

(The coin drops into the cup. The coin's inertia, or resistance to a change in motion, keeps it from moving with the card.)

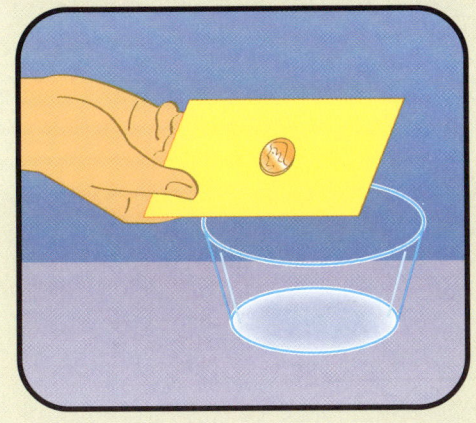 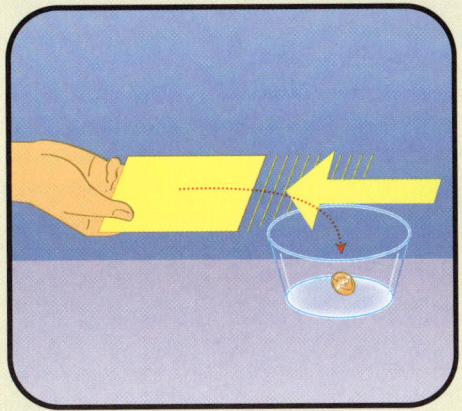

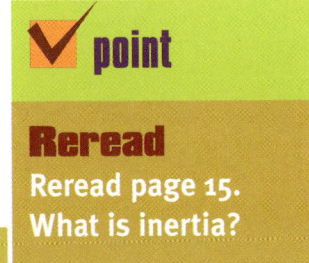

✓ point

Reread
Reread page 15.
What is inertia?

15

CHAPTER 3

Newton's Second Law Of Motion

Suppose you are pulling two kindergartners on a sled over the snow. They yell, "Faster! Faster!" How can you grant their wish? Here are two ways:

1. Pull harder.
2. Have one get off the sled.

Whichever way you choose, you have just demonstrated Newton's second law of motion.

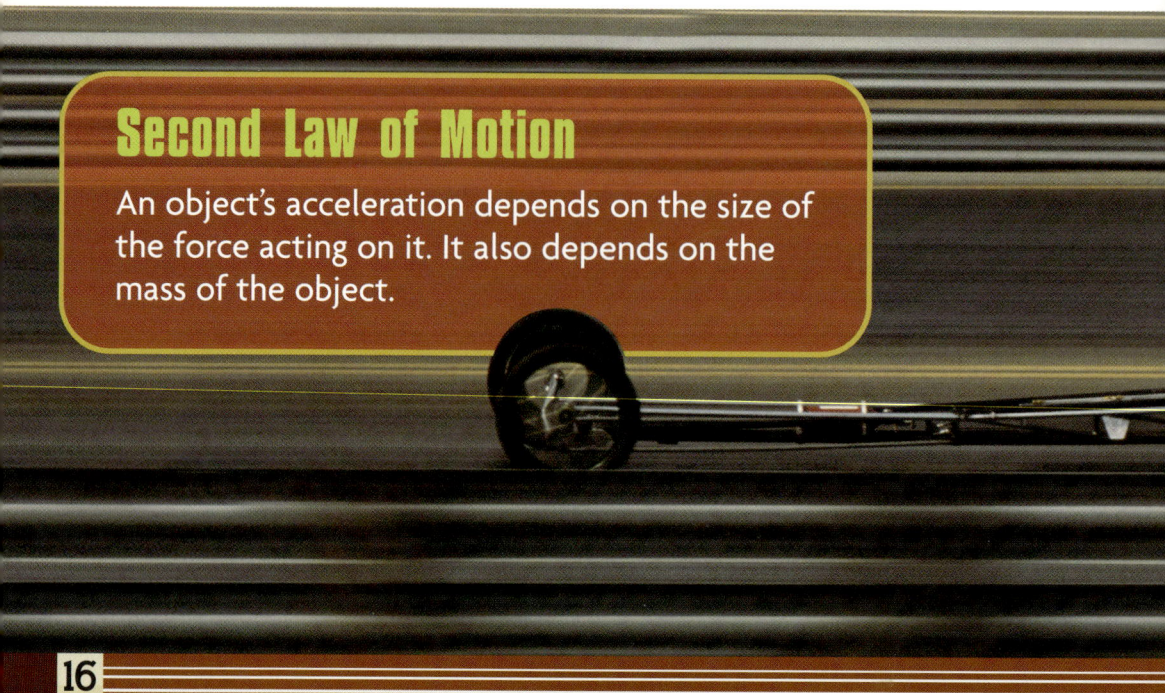

Second Law of Motion

An object's acceleration depends on the size of the force acting on it. It also depends on the mass of the object.

What Is Acceleration?

Acceleration (ak-sel-uh-RAY-shuhn) is how fast an object changes speed or direction or both. You accelerate on your bike when you speed up. You also accelerate when you turn the corner because you change direction. You even accelerate when you slow down. This change in speed is called deceleration.

How does acceleration and Newton's second law apply to the sled? To make the sled go faster, you have two choices.

1. **Give the sled more force.** You can do this by pulling harder, having someone help you pull, or having someone push the sled from behind while you pull.
2. **Reduce the amount of mass that you are pulling.** You can do this by having someone get off the sled.

▼ On your mark, get set, go! A race car accelerates very quickly.

CHAPTER 3

The Math Behind the Law

The second law of motion shows how force, mass, and acceleration are related, or connected, to one another. Newton showed this connection with a math **equation** (ih-KWAY-zhuhn), or expression: **force = mass x acceleration**

To understand how this equation works, think about pushing a shopping cart in a grocery store. The cart has a certain mass. You push it with a certain amount of force to make it accelerate. When you start shopping, the cart is empty and easy to push.

▼ **Less mass makes the cart easier to accelerate.**

NEWTON'S SECOND LAW OF MOTION

By the time you are done shopping, the cart is full of groceries. The full cart has a lot more mass than the empty cart. Will it be as easy to push? According to the equation, if the mass increases and you want the cart to accelerate the same as before, what has to change? The force has to increase, which means you have to push harder.

▼ More mass makes the cart harder to accelerate.

5. Solve This

Use this equation: force = mass x acceleration. How much force is needed to move a filled shopping cart with a mass of 15 kilograms at an acceleration of 5 meters/second^2?

Math ✓ point

Explain how you solved the problem. Remember—to solve for any missing item in an equation, substitute the known values and solve for the missing value.

CHAPTER 3

Units of Force

Every measurement includes a number and a **unit** (YEW-nit). For example, this book is about 24 centimeters (cm) long. The unit is centimeters. Force is measured in units, too. These units are called **newtons** (N) (NOOT-uhnz), named after Isaac.

Let's take another look at the equation for the second law of motion. This time, with the units included:

force (newtons) = mass (kilograms) x acceleration (meters/second^2)

Now, let's put the equation to work.

Suppose a 6-kilogram bowling ball has an acceleration of 2 meters/second^2. How much force did the bowler use to push the ball? You know the mass and acceleration. You want to find the force. Substitute the numbers in the equation.

force = 6 x 2
force = 12 newtons

6. Solve This

A bowling ball is tossed with a force of 40 N. It rolls with an acceleration of 10 meters/second^2. What is the mass of the bowling ball?

Math  point

How did you use the equation to solve the problem? What three variables can be determined using Newton's second law of motion?

CHAPTER 3

Hands-on Experiment
Modeling Newton's Second Law

A spring scale can be used to measure force in newtons (N). Use a spring scale to find out how the second law of motion works.

What You'll Need

spring scale
skateboard
partner

What To Do

1. Hook the spring scale to the empty skateboard.
2. Pull the skateboard with the spring scale. Use a steady pull so that you can read the amount of force used on the scale.
3. Have your partner stand on the skateboard. Pull again with the same force as before. Notice how the skateboard moves (or doesn't).
4. Pull again with enough force to move the skateboard. Read the scale again.

NEWTON'S SECOND LAW OF MOTION

What do you think?

1. What did you change about the skateboard when your partner stood on it?
2. What happened to the amount of force needed to move the skateboard the second time?

CHAPTER 4

Newton's Third Law Of Motion

What happens when you blow up a balloon and let it go? Air rushes out and the balloon flies all over the place. Why does the balloon act this way? It's just following the law—Newton's third law of motion, that is.

The third law of motion means that forces always act in pairs. When one object exerts a force on another object, the second object exerts a force of equal strength on the first object, but in the opposite direction.

Take the balloon. When you let it go, the balloon pushes against the air inside it. The air pushes back with an equal force, but in the opposite direction. The air rushing out of the balloon pushes it forward.

Rockets act much like a balloon. Burning fuel makes gases. The rocket pushes against the gases. As the gases rush out of the rocket, they push against the rocket and send it up, up, and away.

▲ Forces act in pairs. The forces are equal in strength but opposite in direction.

▶ A rocket blasting off is an example of Newton's third law of motion.

Third Law of Motion

For every action, there is an equal and opposite reaction.

25

Conclusion

The world has changed considerably since Isaac Newton presented his laws of motion. Today, engineers use these laws to determine how much force is needed to boost a rocket ship into space. His laws are used to design cars, trains, and airplanes. In fact, these machines could not have been invented without understanding the laws of motion.

Even things that don't move depend on Newton's laws of motion. Builders of bridges and skyscrapers have to understand the forces that will be put on these structures.

◀ Newton's book, *The Mathematical Principles of Natural Philosophy*, explained his laws of motion and gravity to the public.

Newton's laws have led to new and improved sports equipment, too. And athletes can improve their game by understanding the laws of motion. But the next time you're playing in a championship basketball game, do your thinking about Newton's laws before you walk on the court.

Time Line of Sir Isaac Newton's Life

1642	Isaac Newton born in Woolsthorpe, England
1661	Enters Trinity College, Cambridge
1668	Creates reflecting telescope
1669	Becomes professor of mathematics at Trinity College
1686	Presents his laws of motions and law of universal gravitation
1689	Serves as Cambridge's representative to Parliament
1696	Becomes warden of the London Mint; helps figure out new money system
1703	Elected president of the Royal Society, a scientific organization
1705	Becomes Sir Isaac Newton
1727	Newton dies in London; first scientist to be buried at Westminster Abbey

 point

Make Connections

Give an example of how you use each one of Newton's laws of motion in your daily life.

Solve This Answers

1. Page 3
a. Uranus
b. 90
Math Checkpoint
a. Round 84.01 to 80 and multiply by 3 to get an estimate of 240. That is close to the length of time Pluto's orbit takes, 247.7 Earth years.
b. Use compatible numbers to estimate. 0.24 is about 1/4 and 365 days in a year is about 360. 1/4 of 360 is 90.

2. Page 5
a. ∠
b. acute angle
Math Checkpoint
A 75-degree angle, as stated in text, is an acute angle.

3. Page 5
About 80 miles (128 km)
Math Checkpoint
You need a ruler to solve this problem.

4. Page 7
a. 7,950 pounds on Uranus
b. 722 = x
   .38   1
   .38x = 722
   x = 1,900 pounds on Earth

Math Checkpoint
a. Multiplication
b. Cross-multiplication, then division

5. Page 19
75 N
Math Checkpoint
Substituted numbers for mass and acceleration into the equation Force = 15 x 5; Force = 75 N

6. Page 20
The bowling ball weighs four kilograms (about nine pounds). Substitute numbers for force and accelerations into the equation and solve for mass, so mass = force/acceleration. Mass = 40/10; mass = 4 kg
Math Checkpoint
The variables of force, mass, and acceleration can be determined using Newton's second law of motion.

7. Page 27
Clarence's marble has a faster average speed at 8 ft. per second. 24/3=8; 45/9=5
Math Checkpoint
If the marbles have the same mass, Clarence used greater force.

Glossary

acceleration   (ak-sel-uh-RAY-shuhn) an increase in speed (page 17)

equation   (ih-KWAY-zhuhn) a statement in mathematics that two quantities are equal (page 18)

force   (FORS) something that moves a body or stops or changes its motion (page 6)

friction   (FRIK-shuhn) a slowing force caused by two objects rubbing against each other (page 10)

gravity   (GRAHV-ih-tee) force of attraction between objects (page 6)

inertia   (ih-NUR-shuh) resistance to a change in motion (page 15)

mass   (MAS) the amount of matter in an object (page 13)

newton   (NOOT-uhn) a unit of force (page 20)

optics   (OP-tikz) the science of light (page 5)

orbit   (OR-bit) the path one space object takes to move around another (page 2)

speed   (SPEED) the measure of distance over a period of time (page 10)

unit   (YEW-nit) a fixed quantity or amount that is used as a standard of measurement (page 20)

Index

acceleration, 16–20

action and reaction forces, 24–26

equation, 18–20

force, 6–10, 12–20, 22–24, 26, 28

friction, 10, 13–14

Galilei, Galileo, 8–9

gravity, 6–7, 12, 14, 28

inertia, 14–15

knighthood, 6

law of universal gravitation, 6, 29

mass, 13, 15–20, 23, 27

Newton, Isaac, 2, 4–6, 8, 11–12, 15–18, 22, 24–29

Newton, Isaac (father), 4

Newton, Hannah, 4

newton (unit of force), 20, 22

optics, 5–6

orbit, 2–3, 6

Parliament, 29

The Mathematical Principles of Natural Philosophy, 28

reflecting telescope, 6, 29

solar system, 2, 7

speed, 9–10, 12–14, 17, 27

Trinity College, 5, 29

weight, 7

Woolsthorpe, England, 4–5, 29

Woolsthorpe Manor, 4